FISH LIVE IN WATER

By Sarah Ridley

IN THE ANIMAL KINGDOM

WAYLAND

www.waylandbooks.co.uk

First published in Great Britain in 2019
by Wayland

Copyright © Hodder and Stoughton,
2019

Editor: Sarah Peutrill
Designer: Lisa Peacock

ISBN: 978 1 5263 0936 5

Printed and bound in China

Wayland, an imprint of
Hachette Children's Group
Part of Hodder and Stoughton
Carmelite House
50 Victoria Embankment
London EC4Y 0DZ
An Hachette UK Company
www.hachette.co.uk
www.hachettechildrens.co.uk

FSC
MIX
Paper from
responsible sources
FSC® C104740
www.fsc.org

Picture credits: aquapix/Shutterstock: 6. blickwinkel/Alamy: 21b.
baptiste le bouil/Shutterstock: 11. Jane Burton/Nature PL: 19t.
Rich Carey/Shutterstock: 13t. George Clerk/istockphoto: 14.
Brandon Cole/Nature PL: 8. crisod/istockphoto: 12.
Damsea/Shutterstock: 9b, 23t. enzosub/Shutterstock: 3b, 17t.
Jeff Feverston/Shutterstock: 7. frantisekhojdysz/Shutterstock: 20b.
Daniel Huebner/Shutterstock: 2b, 13b. Alex Mustard/Nature PL: 18,
19c, 21t, 23b. NaluOhoto/istockphoto: 16-17. Krzysztof Odziomek/
Shutterstock: 2t, 22t. Doug Perrine/Nature PL: 19b.
Napat Polchoke/istockphoto: 15t. Dave Roberts/SPL: 10.
Ian D M Robertson/Shutterstock: 3t, 23c. Masahiro Suzuki/Shutterstock:
22b. Tatyana Vyc/Shutterstock: front cover. Richard Whitcombe/
Shutterstock: 9t. wildestanimal/Shutterstock: 15b, 20t.
Yoshinori/Shutterstock: 1.

CONTENTS

The animal kingdom

Scientists sort all living things on Earth into five huge groups called kingdoms. All the animals belong in the animal kingdom.

The animal kingdom is divided into two very large groups. The invertebrates are animals without a backbone and the vertebrates are animals with a backbone.

ANIMAL KINGDOM

INVERTEBRATES

Then we divide the vertebrates up again, into five large groups: fish, amphibians, reptiles, birds and mammals.

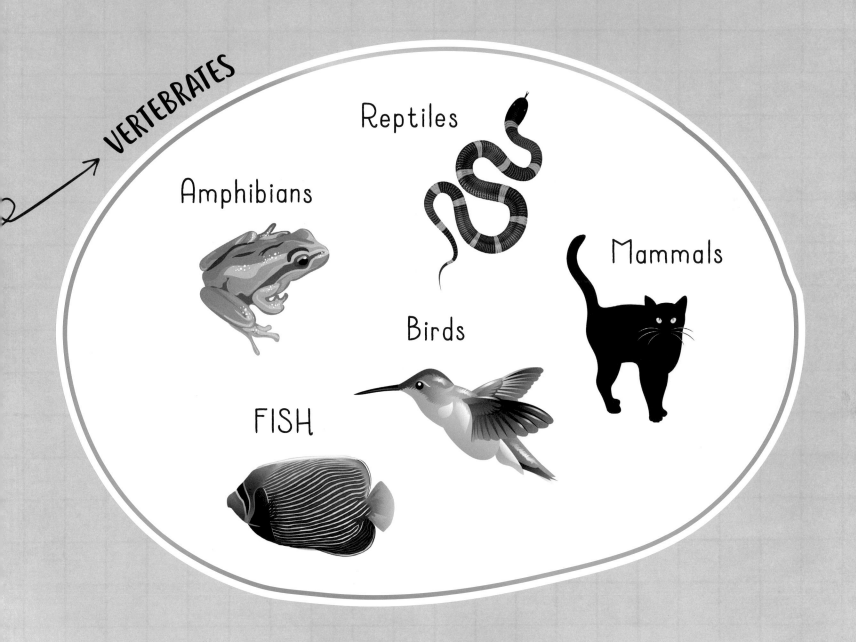

VERTEBRATES

Reptiles

Amphibians

Mammals

Birds

FISH

Read on to find out what makes an animal a fish.

All fish live in water

Fish live in seas and oceans, rivers, streams, lakes and ponds. As water covers three-quarters of planet Earth, that's a lot of homes for fish.

Some fish swim together in shoals to keep safe.

This brown trout is swimming along a riverbed on its own.

Almost all fish are cold-blooded. This means their bodies are the same temperature as the water surrounding them.

Fish have lived on Earth for about 530 million years.

There are three main groups of fish

Pacific hagfish

Fish can be divided into three main groups.
The fish in the first group have no jaw and
include lampreys and hagfish.

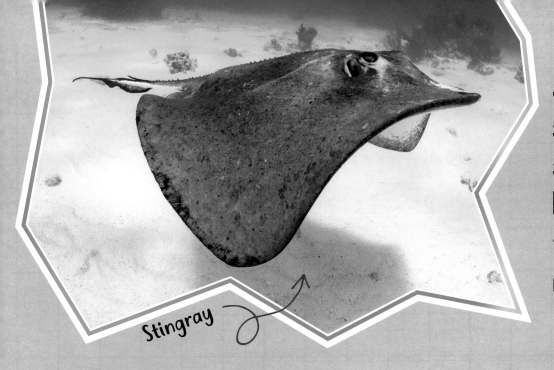

Stingray

Sharks, rays and skates are in the second group. They all have a skeleton made from bendy cartilage, rather than bone.

Fish with a bony skeleton make up the third group. There are over 20,000 different species, or types, of bony fish.

Jellyfish, starfish, cuttlefish and shellfish are NOT fish.

Fish have skeletons

Most fish have a skeleton made of bone. It protects the soft bits of the body and supports the muscles.

Colour X-ray of a fish's skeleton

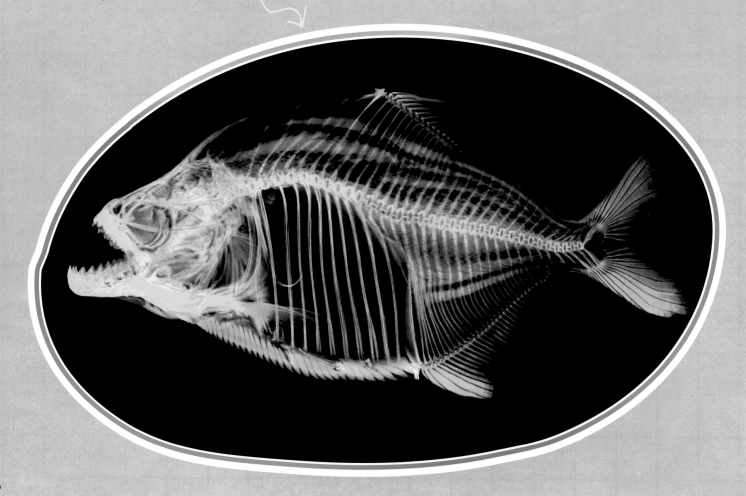

Other fish, including sharks, rays and lampreys, have a skeleton made of cartilage. Cartilage is more bendy than bone and weighs less.

What is your skeleton made of?

Tiger sharks

Most fish have fins

Fins

Fish have fins to stop them rolling over and to help them to swim. Fins help fish, like this pike, to twist and turn, go forwards and slow down.

The streamlined shape of a fish's body lets it slip through water.

Blackfin barracuda

Most fish have a swim bladder – a bag of air inside the body – that helps the fish stay afloat.

Flying fish stretch out their wide fins to glide through the air and escape hunters.

Most fish have scales

Most fish are covered in flat scales. These small, hard plates protect the fish's body.

Which other group of animals has skin covered in scales?

14

This photo shows
fish scales up close.

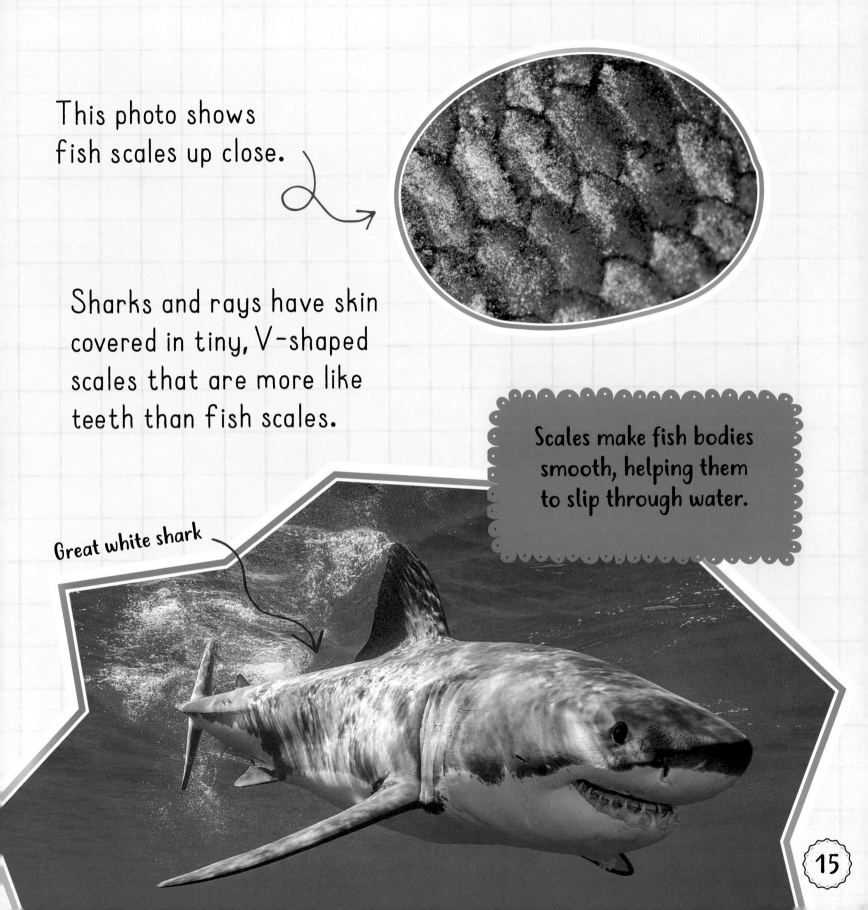

Sharks and rays have skin
covered in tiny, V-shaped
scales that are more like
teeth than fish scales.

Scales make fish bodies
smooth, helping them
to slip through water.

Great white shark

Fish breathe underwater

A shark has gill slits.

Like all animals, fish need to breathe to stay alive. Unlike us, a fish has gills on each side of its body to do this.

Gills under
this flap

Yellow tang

Water enters the fish's mouth
and passes over the gills. There
the gills remove oxygen from the
water before the water leaves
through the gill flaps or slits.

How do you
breathe?

Fish lay eggs

Almost all fish lay eggs. These male and female snappers have released a cloud of eggs and sperm into the sea.

Most fish eggs and young become food for other animals.

Tiny fish grow inside the eggs.

Tiny trout with yolk sac

Seahorse

Trout egg

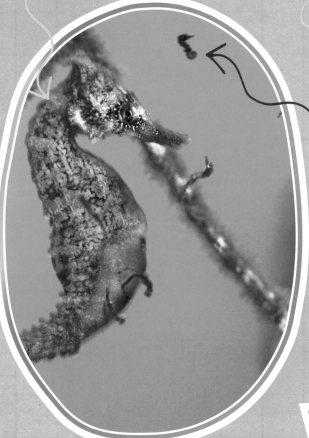

Baby seahorse

Some fish protect their eggs and young. The male seahorse keeps his eggs safe inside his pouch and then gives birth to tiny seahorses.

Lemon shark and pup

The lemon shark gives birth to live young, called pups.

Fish find food in water

Most fish eat other fish. These sailfish work together to catch and eat smaller fish.

Nostril

The hammerhead shark hunts fish and octopuses. It uses its nostrils to sniff them out.

Other types of fish eat tiny plants and animals. Manta rays sieve them out of the water.

A pike will eat any fish smaller than itself, as well as insects and frogs.

Fish are all shapes and sizes

The enormous whale shark only eats tiny fish, plants and animals.

These small clownfish live safely among the stinging tentacles of sea anemones.

A flounder hides at the bottom of the sea. This flatfish has both its eyes on the top of its body.

A leafy sea dragon is the perfect shape for hiding in seaweed.

Garden eels live in burrows in the sea floor.

Glossary

backbone A row of small bones that are connected together to form the spine.

cartilage A bendy, strong body tissue.

egg A round or oval object laid by a female fish, bird or reptile.

fin A thin part of a fish's body that it uses to steer itself and to move.

gill Part of the body of a fish that absorbs oxygen from water, allowing the fish to breathe.

sea anemone A simple invertebrate (animal without a backbone) with stinging tentacles.

skeleton The supporting structure of an animal's body.

species A kind of living thing, such as a brown trout.

sperm A male reproductive cell. The word can also mean the fluid containing sperm cells.

streamlined Having a shape that allows an object or animal to move easily through water or air.

tentacle A long, bendy part of the body of some animals. Anemones use their tentacles to kill and capture tiny animals to eat.

young Another word for animal babies.

X-rays A photo made by X-rays, a type of invisible ray that can pass through objects, allowing us to see bones or body organs inside the body.

Index